MW01101638

E S

G O O D   P R A C T I C E

MAINTAINING
YOUR PC

ABOUT THIS BOOK

Maintaining Your PC is an easy-to-follow guide to the wealth of technical resources contained in Symantec's maintenance software for the PC, Norton SystemWorks™ 2000.

ALL MACHINERY NEEDS MAINTENANCE during its working life, and the PC is no exception. *Maintaining Your PC* provides an introduction to Norton SystemWorks 2000, which is a suite of utilities, tools, and controls designed to help your PC maintain its optimum performance, and to prevent small problems becoming large and damaging ones. Norton SystemWorks contains everything you'll need for organizing the programs and data on your hard drive. You'll be able to remove redundant software safely, protect your computer against viruses, have SystemWorks monitor many aspects of your PC's activities, and perform low-level system checks on fundamental aspects of your system that could not be reached as easily by any other means. Generally, Norton SystemWorks is the ideal set of tools to keep your PC healthy.

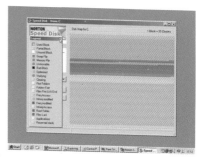

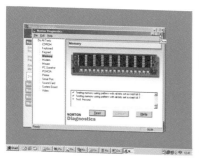

Each chapter of the book can stand alone, so you can choose either to work through the book in sequence or simply go straight to a section that interests you.

The chapters and the subsections present the information using step-by-step sequences. Virtually every step is accompanied by an illustration showing how your screen should look at each stage.

The book contains several features to help you understand both what is happening and what you need to do.

Cross-references are shown in the text as left- or right-hand page icons: ◁ and ▷. The page number and the reference are shown at the foot of the page.

In addition to the step-by-step sections, there are boxes that explain a feature in detail, and tip boxes that provide alternative methods. Finally, at the back, you will find a glossary of common terms, and a comprehensive index.

ESSENTIAL DK COMPUTERS

GOOD PRACTICE

MAINTAINING YOUR PC

JOHN WATSON

A Dorling Kindersley Book

Dorling Kindersley
LONDON, NEW YORK, SYDNEY, DELHI,
PARIS, MUNICH, and JOHANNESBURG

Produced for Dorling Kindersley Limited by
Design Revolution, Queens Park Villa,
30 West Drive, Brighton, East Sussex BN2 2GE

EDITORIAL DIRECTOR Ian Whitelaw
SENIOR DESIGNER Andy Ashdown
PROJECT EDITOR John Watson
DESIGNER Paul Bowler

MANAGING EDITOR Adele Hayward
SENIOR MANAGING ART EDITOR Nigel Duffield
DTP DESIGNER Jason Little
PRODUCTION CONTROLLER Michelle Thomas
US EDITORS Gary Werner and Margaret Parrish

First American Edition, 2001

00 01 02 03 04 05 10 9 8 7 6 5 4 3 2 1

Published in the United States by Dorling Kindersley Publishing, Inc.
95 Madison Avenue, New York, New York, 10016

A Cataloging-in-Publication record is available from the
Library of Congress.

ISBN 0-7894-7292-9

Color reproduced by Colourscan, Singapore
Printed in Italy by Graphicom

See our complete
catalog at
www.dk.com

CONTENTS

NORTON SYSTEMWORKS

If you've ever wished that you had a computer engineer onsite to solve your computer's impenetrable challenges, Norton SystemWorks comes the closest to filling that role.

WHAT IS NORTON SYSTEMWORKS?

Norton SystemWorks is produced by Symantec Corporation and is made up of a collection of utilities that have been available separately in different guises for a number of years. With the release of Norton SystemWorks 2000, Symantec has integrated these utilities into a very large and very powerful suite of programs for maintaining your PC.

This integration is a natural response to the developments in computer software in recent years. Programs, as well as operating systems, have become far larger, more complex, more demanding of resources, and less manageable for the home and small-to-medium office user.

SystemWorks now provides the tools to help control and manage your system.

WHAT CAN I DO WITH SYSTEMWORKS?

● The common and essential daily tasks carried out on a PC of adding, changing, and deleting data create problems that are usually invisible in their effect. One of these undesirable effects fragments file storage across the hard drive, slowing it down and wasting space. Among SystemWorks' features is the reorganization of your hard drive for maximum efficiency.

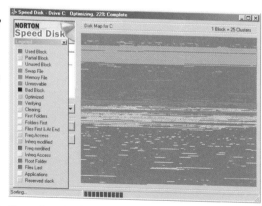

Norton SystemWorks provides a colorful and informative disk map of your hard drive while it restructures your data 🗋.

25 **Speed Disk**

LAUNCHING NORTON SYSTEMWORKS

Norton SystemWorks has been called the "program of all programs," and approaching such a highly regarded piece of software could be seen as a daunting prospect. However, despite the fact that the capabilities of Norton SystemWorks far exceed those of many applications that you may have on your computer, it is nevertheless launched as easily as any other program.

LAUNCHING WITH THE START MENU

● If you are running Windows 95 or 98 and you have already installed Norton SystemWorks on your PC, begin by clicking on the **Start** button at the bottom left of the screen. When you installed Norton SystemWorks, a shortcut was placed toward the top of the pop-up menu.

● Click on the System-Works shortcut on this menu, and SystemWorks opens on-screen.

LAUNCHING WITH THE SHORTCUT ICON

● A further shortcut was created when you installed Norton SystemWorks, and this was placed on the Windows Desktop.

● Double-clicking on this icon is an alternative method of launching SystemWorks.

THE SYSTEMWORKS INTEGRATOR

There are broadly two types of PC software. The first is based on a document window, such as Microsoft Word and Excel. The second type is based on a menu window, and it is to this group that Norton SystemWorks belongs. In SystemWorks, the window containing the principal menu options is known as the Integrator, and all SystemWorks tools are available from this window.

BUTTONS KEY

❶ Home
Clicking on this button from any part of SystemWorks returns you to the Integrator.
❷ LiveUpdate
Clicking this button connects you to Symantec's website. Among the many features available on this site is the opportunity to update the list of viruses that your system is protected against. If necessary, you can also submit files that might be infected with a virus directly to Symantec.
❸ LiveAdvisor
LiveAdvisor is a feature that acts as your personal information agent. LiveAdvisor checks with Symantec for messages about product information, software upgrades, various updates, and technical tips for the Symantec products you register.

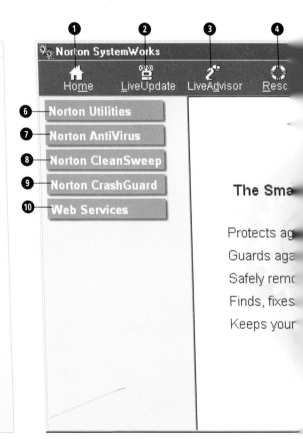

NORTON SYSTEMWORKS HELP

The fact that Norton SystemWorks is an integration of several different utilities is very apparent in the Help screens that are available. Each of the different parts of SystemWorks has its own separate Help section. A slight disadvantage is that you first need to know which feature contained in SystemWorks is likely to contain the procedures you need before you can look up the subject.

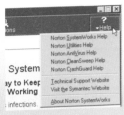

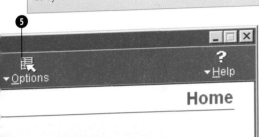

Home

...ton SystemWorks

...t Way to Keep Your Computer Working

...virus infections.

...system crashes and screen freezes.

...programs and files.

...prevents Windows problems.

...ware drivers and software up-to-date.

NORTON SystemWorks2000

BUTTONS KEY

4 Rescue
This button is a shortcut to creating a set of rescue disks to revive your computer.

5 Options
Access the many controls offered by SystemWorks.

6 Norton Utilities
Tools to use on your hard drive are contained here.

7 Norton AntiVirus
Everything you need to check for and to prevent viruses.

8 Norton CleanSweep
Prevent your hard drive from being filled with unnecessary data by removing it safely.

9 Norton CrashGuard
Monitor your software for impending crashes and take avoiding action.

10 Web Services
Connect immediately to Symantec's website for all the latest information and upgrades.

NORTON UTILITIES

Norton Utilities has been an indispensable tool for the experienced computer user for several years. Its inclusion in SystemWorks 2000 means that it is now available to everyone.

HOW NORTON UTILITIES CAN HELP

Norton Utilities contains virtually every imaginable tool that you are likely to need to unearth and repair software problems, improve the performance of your PC, monitor the way your computer is functioning to prevent potential problems from becoming serious, and to troubleshoot hardware problems. The utilities are grouped into four sections: Find and Fix Problems, Improve Performance, Preventive Maintenance, and Troubleshoot.

LAUNCHING NORTON UTILITIES

● Norton Utilities is available via the first button on the left-hand panel of buttons in the Norton SystemWorks Integrator. Click on it to view the options that it contains.

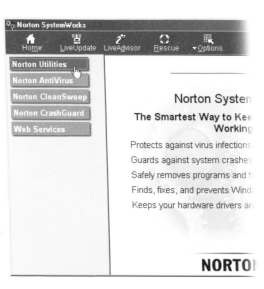

FIND AND FIX PROBLEMS

Find and Fix Problems makes up the first collection of utilities, and includes Norton System Check, Norton WinDoctor, Norton Disk Doctor, and the UnErase Wizard. If they are not displayed, click on the **Find and Fix Problems** button.

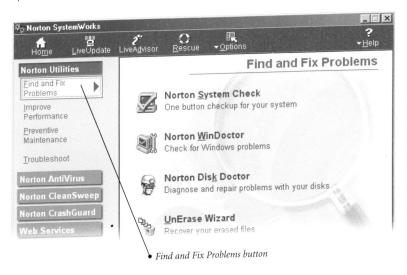

Find and Fix Problems button

NORTON SYSTEM CHECK

● System Check is the first option in Norton Utilities, possibly because you may need to access it quickly when you think you have a problem. System Check is designed to locate disk problems at the time they arise. Click on the **Norton System Check** button panel to begin running the utility.

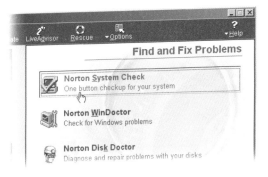

● The System Check Welcome screen appears giving a brief account of what System Check will do. Welcome screens appear in the majority of cases when an option is selected in Norton SystemWorks. After reading what these screens contain, you can place a check mark in the check box next to Don't show me this again to prevent the screen from reappearing, and then click on Continue.

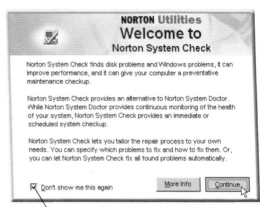

Click here to prevent this window from reappearing

● The **Norton System Check Wizard** dialog box opens and contains four analysis categories: **Find disk problems**, **Find Windows problems**, **Improve performance**, and **Preventative maintenance**. In this example, the default selection of **Find disk problems** is selected.
  ● Click on **Next**.

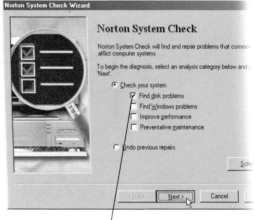

Find disk problems ●

● The **Norton System Check Wizard** begins analyzing the condition of the hard drive (or drives, if you have more than one) as well as checking whether any files are missing and then attempting to establish where they are.

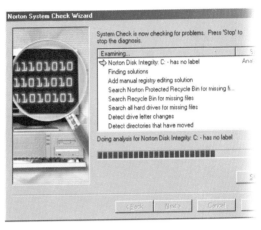

● The **Wizard** works its way through the list of different tasks, and inserts a check mark at the completion of each one. At the end of the process, the text above and below the checklist changes, and the **Next** button becomes active, which you can click to view the results.

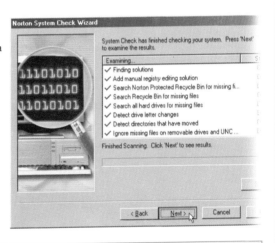

SCHEDULING NORTON SYSTEM CHECK

To schedule System Check, click **Options** in the Integrator, select Norton Utilities. In the **Norton Utilities Options** dialog box, click on the **System Check Scheduler** tab. Click on the drop-down menu next to **How Often?** and select the frequency from **Daily**, **Weekly**, or **Monthly**.

● The **Wizard's** results
window shows the number
of errors found. The details
can be seen by clicking on
Finish. Naturally, if no
errors are found, you will
be informed of the fact and
clicking on **Finish** will end
the System Check session.

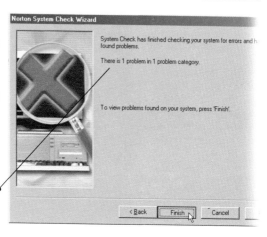

System Check results

● The results window
displays the problem in a
checklist and assigns a
severity rating. In this
example, one problem has
been found with a severity
rating of **High**, but it can
be corrected by clicking on
Repair. If more than one
problem had been found, it
is possible either to click on
Repair All to correct all of
the problems that have
been found, or to correct
individual problems, one at
a time, by highlighting
them in turn and clicking
on **Repair**.

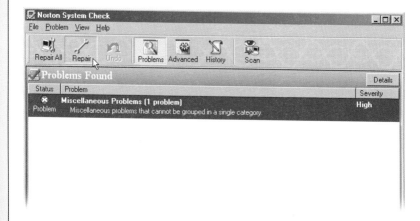

● In the **Automated Repair** dialog box, the options are to let System Check select the best method of repair, or to choose your own solution. It is highly advisable to let System Check choose the repair method, particularly if you are new to SystemWorks.

● As this is the default option, simply click on **OK**.

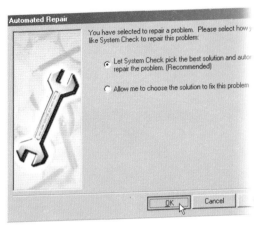

● In this example, System Check has elected to run Norton Disk Doctor to fix the problem, and a checklist shows the different tests that are carried out and how far they have progressed.

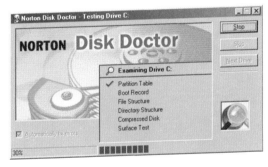

● A **Repair** progress box opens with a meter charting the repair, which is carried out almost instantly and is replaced by an information box confirming that the repair has been successful.

● Click on **OK**.

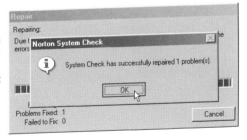

● The checklist window containing the problems reappears. This window can now be closed by clicking on the **Close** button in the top right corner of the window.

NORTON WINDOCTOR

Problems that are specific to the Windows operating system are handled in Norton SystemWorks by Norton WinDoctor. These may be problems in either the Windows registry, which is a database used by Windows to store information about your computer's configuration, or the problems may be in the system files, which are at the heart of the Windows operating system, or in the programs on your PC.

● Launch **Norton WinDoctor** by clicking on its button panel. A Welcome screen appears, which again can be prevented from reappearing by checking the **Don't show me this again** check box, and closed by clicking on **Continue**.

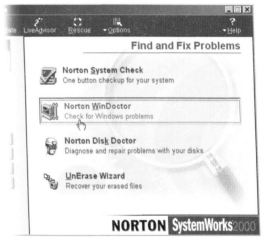

● The **Norton WinDoctor Wizard** dialog box contains three options. The first is to perform the standard WinDoctor tests, the second is to select specific tests to be run, and the third is to view a log of past repairs, and to reverse them if necessary. These last two options need to be practiced before they can be used with confidence.

● Accept the default selection to **Perform all Norton WinDoctor tests** and click on **Next**.

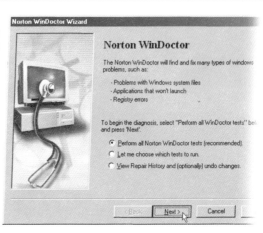

● The **Norton WinDoctor Wizard** window opens and, as the tests are carried out, a checklist gives details of which parts of the software are being examined. A series of progress bars is displayed while the tests are being completed.

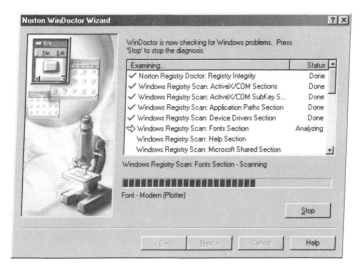

● When the tests are finished, WinDoctor informs you above the checklist.

● Click on **Next** to see the results of WinDoctor's analysis.

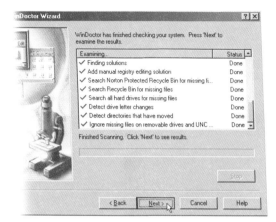

● In the outmoded computer used to illustrate these examples, WinDoctor has found numerous problems in two different categories that need to be corrected.

● Click on **Finish** to see the details.

The number of problems found is shown here

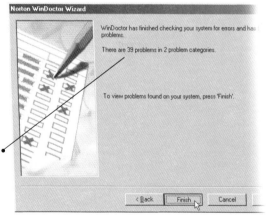

THE PROBLEM TYPES IN WINDOCTOR

Missing program files: In this case, a file, or files, that is required to run a program cannot be found.

ActiveX/COM related problems: This refers to an entry in the registry that points to a piece of software, but is invalid.

Registry related problems: This relates to the previous problem but here a shortcut points to a file that is nonexistent.

● The **Problems Found** panel shows that there are 13 problems in the part of the Windows Registry that relate to ActiveX/Com entries. ActiveX is a technology that makes it easier for applications to share controls. The controls have access to the Windows operating system on your PC and, as a result, carry the risk of damaging software or data on your machine. Norton Win-Doctor looks for evidence that your machine could be damaged.

● The second category of problems results from software having been removed from the machine, but the associated shortcuts have been left behind.

● Severity ratings are again applied to the problems. WinDoctor can easily handle these two classes of problem, so you can click on the **Repair All button**.

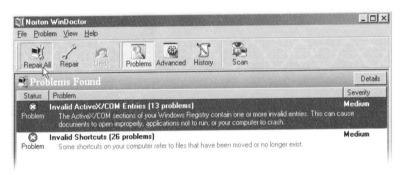

● A panel appears confirming the actions that WinDoctor is about to carry out.

● Click on **Yes**.

● A **Repair** panel appears and is very quickly replaced by a panel confirming the success of the repairs. In this case, all the errors have been repaired. Click on **OK**. (The **Problems Found** panel reappears, which can be closed by clicking on its **Close** button at top right.)

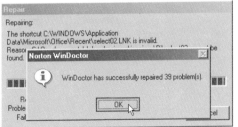

UNDOING NORTON WINDOCTOR REPAIRS

After WinDoctor has carried out its repairs, the occasion may arise when you need to reverse WinDoctor's actions. To do so, click on **Norton WinDoctor** in the Integrator, and in the **Norton WinDoctor Wizard** dialog box click in the radio button alongside **View Repair History and** (optionally) **undo changes**, then click on **Finish**. In the **Repair History** panel of the following window, scroll down to the repair to be undone, click on it to select it, and click on the **Undo** button in the **Tools** menu bar.

NORTON DISK DOCTOR

● The tests carried out by Norton Disk Doctor are designed to diagnose, and then repair, a number of aspects of your hard drive including how it is partitioned, how the files and directories are structured, and the physical condition of the drive.

● Norton Disk Doctor is launched in the usual way by clicking on its button panel. (A Welcome screen again appears and can be closed in the usual way.)

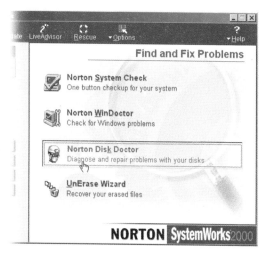

● Norton Disk Doctor can be customized to perform its repairs in several ways. The customization options are accessible by clicking on the **Options** button in the Disk Doctor window.

● The default setting is for Disk Doctor to ask that any given repair should be confirmed before it is carried out. The alternatives are for repairs to be carried out automatically, to be skipped, or to be customized.

● Once you are familiar with using Disk Doctor, you can select options as desired, but for the moment click on **OK**.

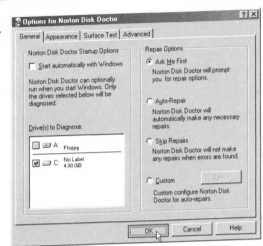

● After making sure that the correct drive is checked (in this case, C:), click on **Diagnose** to begin the tests to be carried out by Disk Doctor.

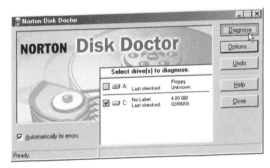

WHAT DISK DOCTOR EXAMINES

The Disk Doctor looks at essential features of your system, including:
Logical Disk Organiz-ation: The operating system organizes the data and records information about the occupied, empty, and damaged areas. Disk Doctor verifies this data.
Cross-Linked Files: When file data from two files is shown as occupying the same area of a disk, Disk Doctor can correct this.
Boot Sector: The sector size and cluster size is recorded in the boot sector. Disk Doctor corrects errors found here and prevents file damage.

● As is characteristic in the way that SystemWorks operates, Disk Doctor works through a checklist of test categories with a progress bar below it.

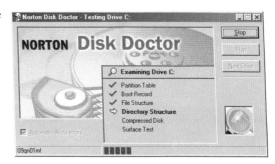

● In this instance, the **Test Results for Drive C:** window shows that Disk Doctor found no problems on the hard drive. Had any problems been found, the repair procedure is similar to what we have seen in, for example, Norton WinDoctor 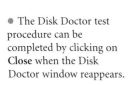.

● Click on **OK** to close the **Test Results** window.

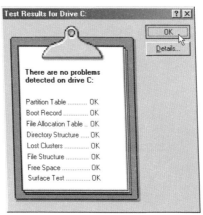

● The Disk Doctor test procedure can be completed by clicking on **Close** when the Disk Doctor window reappears.

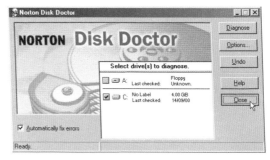

UNERASE WIZARD

● An invisible aspect of SystemWorks is the Norton Protection module, which loads automatically when Windows starts and keeps track of the original names of deleted files, the file types, their size, and how the files were deleted. By using the UnErase Wizard, deleted files can be recovered from within the Protection module where they are retained for between 1 to 999 days.

● **UnErase Wizard** is launched by clicking on its button panel in the SystemWorks Integrator.

● The **UnErase Wizard** window contains two default options, which either find all the protected files on your hard drive or allow you to specify criteria to determine which files are recovered, which is useful when many files could be found.

● In this example, there is only one deleted file to be recovered. Therefore the **Find all protected files on local drives** radio button can be selected because the results will not be overwhelming.

● Click on **Next**.

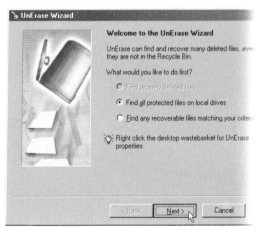

● The UnErase Wizard shows the one protected file and its related information.
● This file can be unerased simply by clicking on **Recover**.

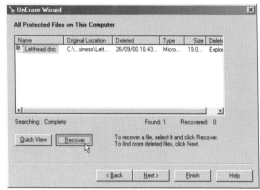

● There is very little that appears to happen other than the file vanishing from the list of protected files. However, it is removed from the Protection module and placed back in its original folder.
● All that is needed now is to click on **Finish**.

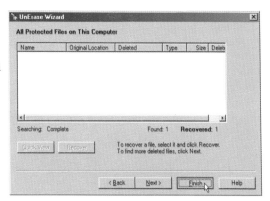

UNERASE WIZARD SHORTCUT MENU

A useful shortcut is available with the Unerase Wizard. Click on **Unerase Wizard** in the Integrator. Click in the radio button next to **Find all protected files on local drives**, and click on **Next**. In the protected files list, select a file and right-click on **Name.** From the pop-up menu, you can select from the following: **Quick View** shows the file's contents; **Recover** performs a normal recovery; **Recover To** relocates the recovered file to a different location; **Delete** removes the file; and **Properties** displays the properties the file.

IMPROVE PERFORMANCE

The Improve Performance section of Norton Utilities contains just two options, which are Speed Disk and the Norton Optimization Wizard.

The main task carried out by Speed Disk is to defragment your hard drive. Files are stored on the hard drive in discrete units called clusters, and, if the clusters in which they are stored are on different parts of the drive, the performance of your PC is slowed down due to the time taken to find and assemble all the relevant pieces into a functioning application.

The Optimization Wizard configures important aspects of your computer to ensure maximum efficiency.

LAUNCHING IMPROVE PERFORMANCE

● The Improve Performance utilities are accessed by clicking on the **Improve Performance** button under the Norton Utilities button.

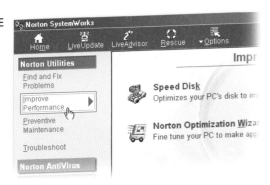

SPEED DISK

● Speed Disk is the first of the two utilities listed in Improve Performance and is launched by clicking on its button panel. (A Welcome screen follows, which can be closed by clicking on **Continue**.)

● The first action carried out by Speed Disk is to check the level of file fragmentation. When done, a **Recommendation** dialog box appears giving the degree of fragmentation together with a method for correcting the problem.

● The radio button for the recommended method is automatically selected, and the process is begun by click on **Start**.

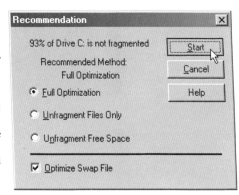

● Speed Disk begins a sorting procedure, and a multicolored **Disk Map** represents the data on your hard drive showing how they are scattered. A key to the data types can be seen by clicking on **Legend** in the left-hand panel.

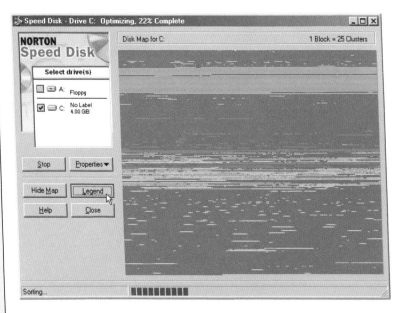

● The length of time taken to defragment a hard drive depends on its size and condition, but the process can easily take more than an hour if this is the first time the drive has been defragmented.

● The Disk Map progressively changes as the data are relocated and reorganized.

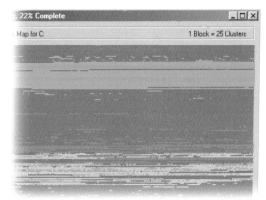

● When Speed Disk has finished, a **Complete** panel informs you of the fact.

● Click on **OK**. The **Disk Map** behind shows the newly ordered contents of your hard drive.

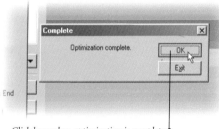

Click here when optimization is complete ●

● Speed Disk performs a final scan of the hard drive. The change in color on the Disk Map while this is happening simply differentiates between used and unused blocks and does not mean that your files have been converted to a different type of file.

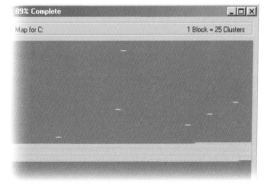

● Once the final scan has been completed, click on the **Close** button of the **Legend** panel to remove it.

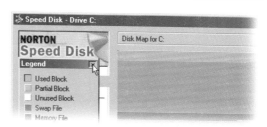

● The Speed Disk window can now be closed by clicking on the **Close** button.

NORTON OPTIMIZATION WIZARD

● The function of the **Norton Optimization Wizard** is to fine-tune the performance of your PC and is launched by clicking on its button panel.

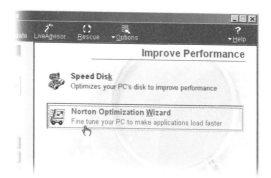

• The Welcome screen refers first to **Swap File Optimization** – setting an efficient size for part of your hard drive that is an extension of random access memory (RAM).

• **Registry Files Optimization** refers to information that is used by Windows and your programs. The Wizard rearranges the storage of the data, again to achieve maximum efficiency.

• Click on **Next** when you have finished reading the Welcome screen.

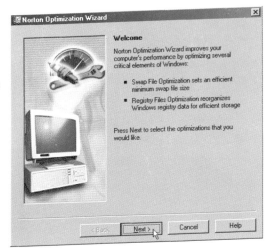

• The first of the two following windows provides further information and informs you whether or not your swap file is configured for maximum efficiency. If it is satisfactorily configured, this window will advise you to leave the swap file as it is, and you can simply click on the **Cancel** button.

• In this case, however, the swap file can be optimized. Make sure that there is a check mark in the **Configure swap file for optimal performance** check box and click on **Next**.

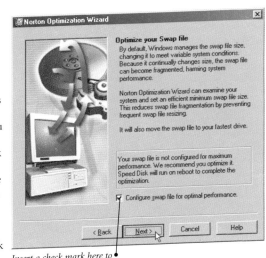

Insert a check mark here to configure the swap file

● The following window
concerns the registry.
Unless the advice that it
contains indicates
otherwise, make sure
there is a check mark in
the **Optimize my Registry**
check box.
● Click on **Next**.

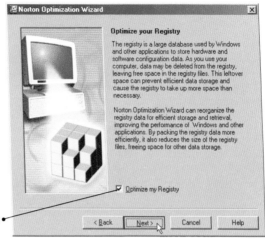

Click here to optimize
the registry

● Now that you have
finished making your
selections, the **Wizard**
summarizes them and
advises you to close all
other programs because
the first action that the
Wizard takes is to reboot
your computer.
● Click on the **Reboot**
button when you have
closed all other programs.
Your computer will reboot
and the Optimization
Wizard performs the
necessary actions.

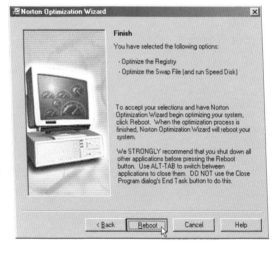

COMPLETING THE OPTIMIZATION PROCESS

● The activities that are now carried out by the Optimization Wizard operate at a very fundamental level of your computer and are performed automatically. This is why it is not possible to illustrate what you will see on your screen while the reboot takes place.

● You will see the Wizard examining your registry, and then an **Optimizing Folders** panel appears, which is identical to the Speed Disk window with its Disk Map ▯. The title bar at the top eventually reads **Optimizing Folders 100%**, but if you are tempted to click on the **Close** button at this point, make sure that

you do not, because the optimization process is beginning.
● Once the process has taken place, the Optimization Wizard reboots your computer again. After the reboot, you are returned to your normal desktop, and Norton SystemWorks has closed itself down.

PREVENTIVE MAINTENANCE

In the standard installation of Norton SystemWorks, there are two options available under Preventive Maintenance: Norton System Doctor, which we

concentrate on here, and the opportunity to make an image of your system data, which is designed to be used if you accidentally format a hard drive.

LAUNCHING PREVENTIVE MAINTENANCE

● The **Preventive Maintenance** element of Norton SystemWorks is launched by clicking its button below Norton Utilities.

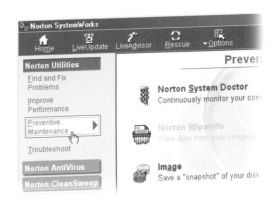

25 **Speed Disk**

NORTON SYSTEM DOCTOR

● Once activated, Norton System Doctor operates continuously and monitors many aspects of your computer via a set of sensors that provide an alert when a problem is detected. Click on the Norton System Doctor button panel to launch this utility. A Welcome screen appears, but once that has been closed by clicking on **Continue**, you will not be able to detect any obvious or immediate change.

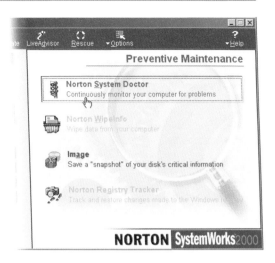

● Although nothing appears to have changed, your screen now contains an added facility in the form of a panel that appears when the cursor approaches its edge. The panel may be concealed along the top edge of the screen, and it can be relocated by dragging it in the same way that the Windows taskbar can be dragged to any of the four sides of the screen.

● In this example, the panel has been moved to the right-hand side of the screen and emerges when the cursor approaches it.

*The **Disk Health** sensor checks the overall health of your hard drive and alerts you when a problem is detected. You can then run the appropriate maintenance utilities to head off serious trouble.* ●

The top-left sensor monitors the amount of free space on your hard drive. The top-right sensor continuously monitors the optimization of your hard drive and displays an alert when the figure drops to 95 percent. ●

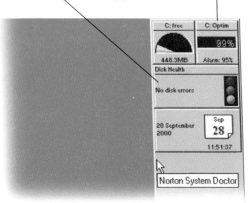

● If you wish to close Norton System Doctor at any time, right-click on an empty section of the panel and select **Close** from the pop-up menu.

● One of the reasons why you may wish to close System Doctor is that on slower computers there may be a performance hit of up to 20 percent when System Doctor is running. This is likely to be more noticeable when you need to run several applications simultaneously.

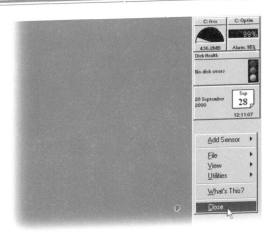

● A dialog box appears asking if you want either to close System Doctor or to minimize it. Click on the appropriate radio button and then click on **OK**.

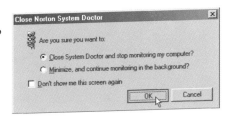

● If you minimize System Doctor, its icon appears in the system tray on the task bar. Hovering the cursor over the tray displays the traffic signals icon of the **Disk Health** sensor.

Adding sensors

You can display several System Doctor sensors on its panel by right-clicking on the panel and selecting **Add Sensor**. A pop-up menu appears containing several categories of sensors, each with its own pop-up menu from which you can select the sensor you wish to display. To remove a sensor from the panel, right-click on it and select **Remove**.

NORTON UTILITIES TROUBLESHOOT

There will inevitably be times when you know, or at least suspect, that there is a problem with one of the pieces of hardware attached to your computer.

Troubleshoot provides you with the option of selecting the peripheral and have Norton Troubleshoot test it to identify whether or not there is a problem.

● **Troubleshoot** is launched by clicking on its button within Norton Utilities.

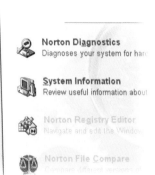

NORTON DIAGNOSTICS

● The diagnostic element within Troubleshoot, **Norton Diagnostics**, is started by clicking on its button panel. (A Welcome screen appears again, which can be closed by clicking on the **Continue** button.)

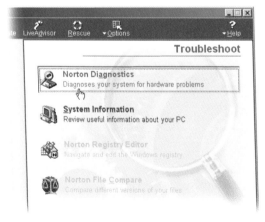

● On the left-hand side of the Norton Diagnostics dialog box is a list of the 13 possible tests that can be carried out. In this example, the **Modem** entry has been clicked.

● Troubleshoot scans the communication ports automatically to locate the modem. After the scan, the modem here has been found on the port called **COM3**.

● When Troubleshoot has found the modem, you can then click on **Test** to begin the diagnostic process.

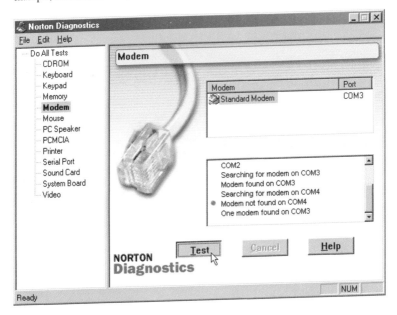

● Troubleshoot checks for the dial tone on the phone line, ensures that the computer and the modem have recognized each other (known as "carrier detect") and that the modem has sent a signal to the computer confirming that it is ready to send a signal, otherwise known as "clear to send" (CTS).

Testing a modem

Before allowing Norton Diagnostics to test a modem, close any programs that are using the modem, or are likely to use it. This includes programs such as Dial-Up Networking, WinFax Pro, and pcANYWHERE, which automatically answers the phone.

● The result of the test is shown at the foot of the checklist box. When the testing has been completed and the results are satisfactory, click on the **Close** button at top right of the dialog box.

● If the modem is found to be faulty, Troubleshoot identifies the problem for you, which will be useful information when consulting an engineer to have the fault corrected.

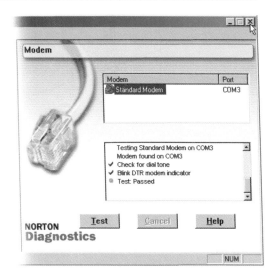

SYSTEM INFORMATION

● A further feature in Troubleshoot, which will be useful when consulting an engineer, is System Information. This identifies all the components of your system together with their current status and performance.

● Click on the **System Information** button panel.

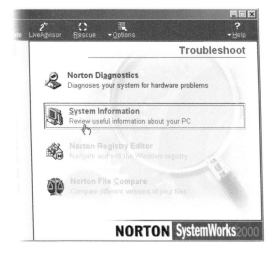

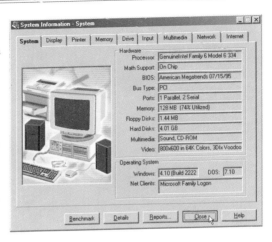

● The information is contained in nine tabs along the top of the **System Information - System** window. Click on the relevant tab to view the information that it contains.

● Your system can also be benchmarked for purposes of comparison by clicking on the **Benchmark** button, and much more technical information can be viewed by clicking on the **Details** button.

● Click on the **Close** button when you have finished viewing the information.

SYSTEM INFORMATION TABS

The **System Information - System** window in Troubleshoot provides a comprehensive account of what your system comprises, and is a further source of information that will be useful when consulting an engineer. When you encounter information that you wish to keep, you can print a report for further reference.

In addition to what we have seen contained under the **System** tab, the other tabs contain the following:

Display: This tab shows the setup of your monitor.

Printer: Identifies your printer and its setup.

Memory: Analyzes how much available memory you have and the amount that is being used by each application that you are currently running.

Drive: Provides information about the amount of free disk space, used disk space, and a detailed list of how much space is being used by each file. You can also benchmark your drive's performance.

Input: Lists the input devices of your computer.

Multimedia: This tab covers the video, audio, and joystick components of your computer.

Network: Shows the network, if you are connected to one.

Internet: Gives details of your internet connection.

NORTON ANTIVIRUS

More than 50,000 viruses are thought to have been released, and they can arrive on a computer from many sources. Norton AntiVirus provides some of the best protection available.

WHAT CAN NORTON ANTIVIRUS DO?

In addition to constantly monitoring your computer system for viruses, Norton AntiVirus also allows you to keep the list of known viruses up-to-date on your computer by downloading lists of viruses from Symantec's website. You can also perform virus scans manually at any time. A further option is to create a set of rescue disks, which you can use if a virus does succeed in penetrating your system.

LAUNCHING NORTON ANTIVIRUS

● **Norton AntiVirus** is launched by clicking on its button in the left-hand panel of the Norton SystemWorks Integrator.
● Click on it to view the options that it contains.

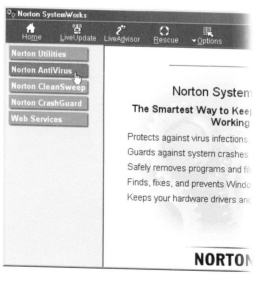

Norton SystemWorks

Home · LiveUpdate · LiveAdvisor · Rescue · ▼Options

Norton Utilities
Norton AntiVirus
Norton CleanSweep
Norton CrashGuard
Web Services

Norton System

The Smartest Way to Keep Working

Protects against virus infections
Guards against system crashes
Safely removes programs and fil
Finds, fixes, and prevents Windo
Keeps your hardware drivers and

NORTON

SYSTEM STATUS

The System Status section of Norton AntiVirus is the maintenance department of the program. You can maintain a current list of viruses together with their characteristics, known as "virus definitions," by downloading the latest information automatically from Symantec's website. You can have Norton AntiVirus scan any part of your computer system for viruses, and create rescue disks.

● Click on the **System Status** button in the left-hand panel if its contents are not already displayed.

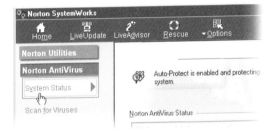

AUTO-PROTECT

● Auto-Protect is a feature of Norton AntiVirus that is operating constantly while your computer is switched on. Auto-Protect works in the background to protect you in several ways. First, by discovering and eradicating any viruses that already exist on your system; second, by preventing your computer from being infected by viruses; and last, by monitoring your system for any viruslike activity that may indicate the presence of an unknown virus.

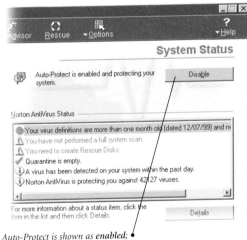

*Auto-Protect is shown as enabled; click on **Disable** to close it*

RUNNING LIVEUPDATE

● LiveUpdate is provided to update the list of viruses that your computer is protected against. Updating is carried out by downloading virus definitions and product updates from the internet.

● Click on the first line of the Status panel that refers to virus definitions, then click on the **Details** button to access LiveUpdate.

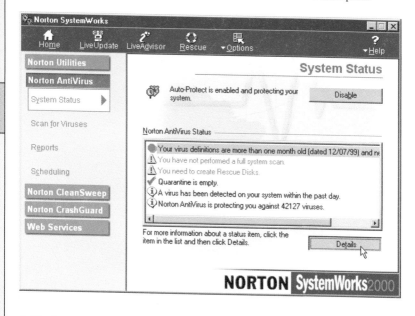

● The **System Status Details** dialog box opens. Click on **Yes** to run LiveUpdate.

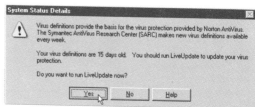

● A Welcome window opens with the option **Find device automatically** already selected.
● Click on **Next**. Live-Update then makes an internet connection if you are not already connected.

● After connecting to Symantec's website, LiveUpdate downloads information about available updates and compares it with the current status of your computer. A progress bar shows the information being retrieved.

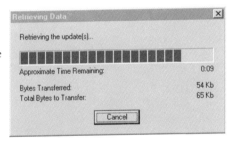

● Once the list of updates has been compiled, you have the opportunity to select which updates you want to download during this session. Here, the **Virus Definitions** option has been selected by clicking in the check box next to that option.
● Click on **Next** when you have made your selections from the list.

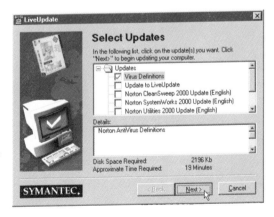

● Once the download has been completed, you can again click on the download options you selected originally to view the results in the **LiveUpdate** window. After clicking on **Virus Definitions**, the **Details** panel shows that the download was successful.

● Click on **Finish**. Live-Update then asks if you want to close your internet connection, and you can click either **Yes** or **No**.

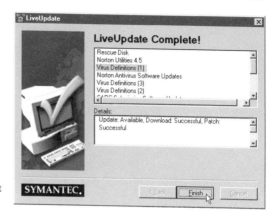

FULL SYSTEM SCAN

● One important element of the analysis that the System Status window provides is to monitor constantly the length of time since you performed a full system scan. This process examines all the software components on your computer for any evidence of a virus infection. Even though you may have Norton AntiVirus constantly enabled, it is still worth performing a regular system scan to ensure a virus-free system.

● Begin the process by highlighting the system scan text in the System Status window.

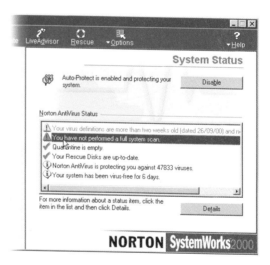

● With the system scan entry selected, click on the **Details** button, which in System Status is the entry point for all further information and activities.

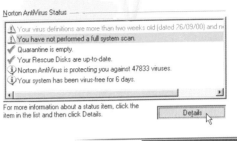

NORTON SystemWorks2000

● Norton AntiVirus uses the opportunity to advise you on the need for a regular weekly scan.
● Click on **Yes** to begin the full system scan.

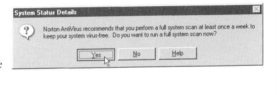

● The Norton AntiVirus scan window opens. The animated graphic runs while the scan is taking place to reassure you that the scan is continuing. A progress meter shows how much of the work remains to be done. The figures below inform you of the actions that have been performed.
● Depending on the size of your system, a full system scan may take as long as one hour to complete.

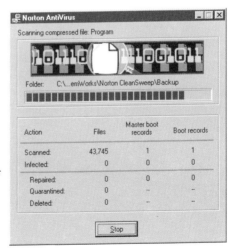

● At the end of the scan, the **Scan Results** dialog box opens. Here, no viruses have been found.

● Close the dialog box by clicking on **Close**.

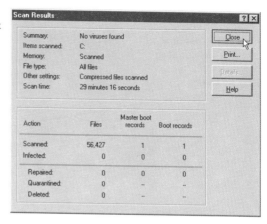

CREATING RESCUE DISKS

● After updating the virus definitions ⌐, you should create, or update, a set of rescue disks to contain the new definitions for use in the event of a virus corrupting your computer.

● Click on **You need to create Rescue Disks**, then click on **Details**.

The Rescue Disk status is reported here

● A dialog box opens in which you have the opportunity to create a set of rescue disks. Click on **Yes** after reading the information that it contains.

● The **Rescue Disk** dialog box automatically selects what type of rescue disk set to create, depending on the hardware configuration of your system. If you have a Zip drive, Norton Rescue will create a rescue disk on that drive. However, in this example, a floppy disk drive has been detected as drive **A:** and the rescue set will be created using that.

● Click on **Create** when the details are correct.

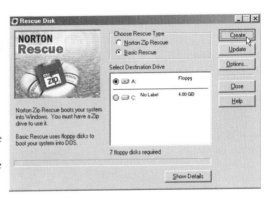

● The **Basic Rescue Disk List** box opens listing the names of the disks that you will need.

● Once you have labeled a set of disks according to the list, click on **OK**.

The list of the different Rescue Disks to be created

● An **Insert Disk** box asks you to insert the first disk. Do so and click on **OK**. This procedure is repeated for each of the rescue disks to be created.

● At the end of the process, a **Basic Rescue Complete** box offers the opportunity to reboot your computer using the set of rescue disks. It is better to find out now whether the set works rather than discovering that the set is flawed when you need to use them.
● If you choose to test the set now, click on **Restart** and follow the on-screen instructions.

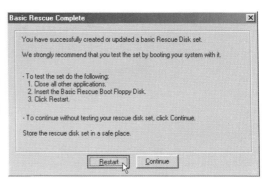

SCANNING FOR VIRUSES

Auto-Protect 📄 monitors your computer constantly for viruses while it is switched on, but there may be times when you wish to perform manual scans.

There is a range of manual scans that are available in Norton AntiVirus, from scanning a single floppy disk to scanning all the drives on your system.

SCANNING A FLOPPY DISK
● Click on **Scan for Viruses** to view the manual scans that Norton AntiVirus provides.

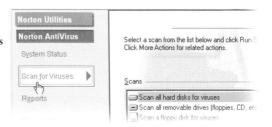

● In this example, a floppy disk is to be scanned. Click on **Scan a floppy disk for viruses**, insert the disk into the floppy disk drive, and click on **Run Scan Now**.

● The scan is carried out and, in this case, the **Norton AntiVirus Repair Wizard** window shows that a common virus, known as the WelcomB virus, has been detected.
● As the Wizard informs you, letting Norton AntiVirus eliminate it automatically is the easiest option. This option is selected by default, so click on **Next**.

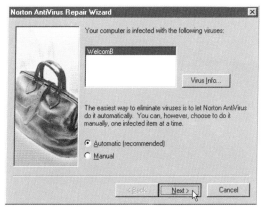

● The **Wizard** congratulates you on eliminating the virus, and after this success, you simply need to click on **Finish**.

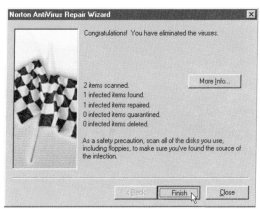

NORTON CLEANSWEEP

Norton CleanSweep contains several features, including removing redundant files that have accumulated on your system and allowing you to create backups of essential data.

WHAT CAN CLEANSWEEP DO?

As you make more and more use of your computer by adding, altering, and deleting programs and files, it is inevitable that quantities of digital litter will be generated in the form of disconnected and redundant data. CleanSweep can remove unwanted files and programs cleanly through its CleanUp feature. Clean-Sweep can also protect your most important files by creating compressed backups that can be retrieved when required by using the Restore Wizard.

LAUNCHING NORTON CLEANSWEEP

● Norton CleanSweep is available via the third button on the Norton SystemWorks Integrator.

● Click on **Norton CleanSweep** to view its contents.

NORTON CLEANSWEEP CLEANUP

Attempting to delete a program by dragging its folder to the Recycle Bin doesn't remove the related files that programs place elsewhere on your computer when you install them. Neither does it remove the configuration settings that programs apply to your system. CleanUp is an invaluable utility that will take care of these related software changes via the Uninstall Wizard, and CleanUp can find and remove remnants of old software by using Fast & Safe Cleanup.

LAUNCHING CLEANUP

● **CleanUp** is the first option within Norton CleanSweeep. Click on its button on the left-hand panel if its contents are not already displayed.

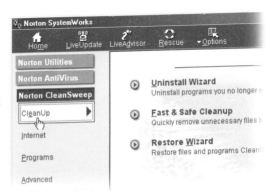

UNINSTALL WIZARD

● With the Uninstall Wizard, you can easily and safely remove unwanted programs and files from you computer to create more disk space.
● Click on the **Uninstall Wizard** button panel to display the Uninstall Wizard dialog box.

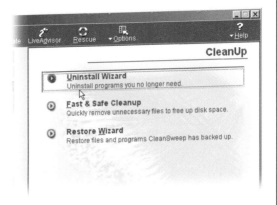

● The Uninstall Wizard uses the contents of the Windows Start menu to display the programs present on your computer.

● You can access the program that you wish to uninstall by first clicking on the plus sign next to **Programs** below the **Start Menu** folder.

*The **Programs** folder*

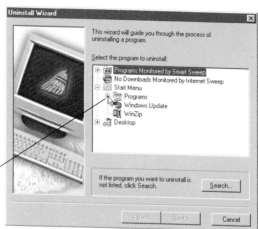

● Scroll down to the program that you are going to uninstall. In this example, Netscape Communicator has been selected.

● Once the program has been highlighted, click on **Next**.

The highlighted program is to be uninstalled

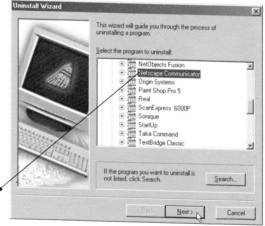

● The Uninstall Wizard analyzes the program to determine the location of the different pieces of software that are associated with it on your system.

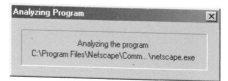

● Rather than erasing the software completely, the Uninstall Wizard will back up the associated files and suggests a default folder as the location for the backup. You have the opportunity to enter an alternative location, but it is better to accept the location suggested by the Wizard.

● Click on **Next**.

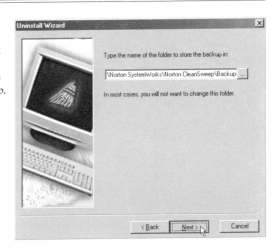

● In rare instances, you may wish to prevent certain files from being deleted, and you are offered the opportunity to confirm each deletion, However, in most cases, this is not necessary. If you don't wish to confirm each deletion, click on **Next** in the window that offers you the opportunity to confirm deletions.

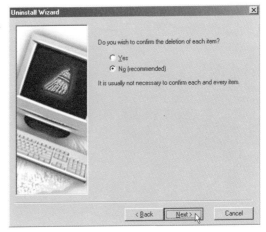

● Once the Uninstall Wizard has gathered the information concerning the program to be deleted, as well as your preferences, you are informed of the amount of data that is to be deleted.

● Now you can click on **Finish** to allow the Uninstall Wizard to begin its work.

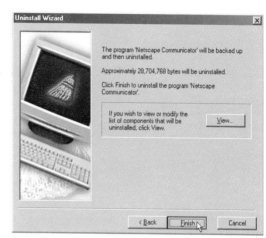

● At the end of the process, the Uninstall Wizard provides you with a more accurate figure of the quantity of data that has been uninstalled.

● The final step is simply to click on **OK**.

Retrieving uninstalled programs
When you need to retrieve a program that has been uninstalled by the Uninstall Wizard, click on **Restore Wizard** in the CleanUp window to be taken through a set of simple steps to reinstate the program on your system.

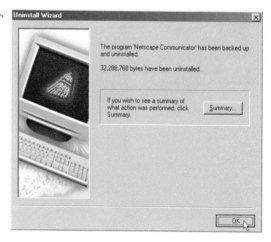

FAST & SAFE CLEANUP

● In addition to uninstalling single programs, you can also remove whole categories of software files from your hard drive by using Fast & Safe Cleanup.

● These categories include temporary files, web pages that you have visited on the internet, known as "cache" files, and the files in the Recycle Bin.

● Click on the Fast & Safe Cleanup button panel to begin the process.

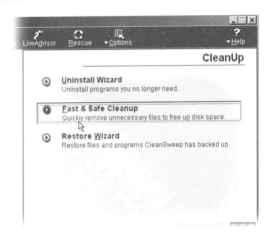

● The program examines your system and displays the results in the Fast & Safe Cleanup dialog box.

● The blue bar at the top of the dialog box shows the amount of free space on your computer while the green bar represents how much more disk space can be freed by deleting unnecessary files.

● Freeing this space is simply carried out by clicking on Clean Now.

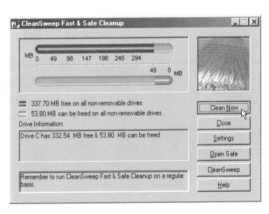

● When the files have been deleted, an information panel confirms the fact, and you can click on OK.

● The Fast & Safe Cleanup dialog box shows a revised representation of the free space on your hard drive, with no space occupied by removable files.

● The process is completed by clicking on **Close**.

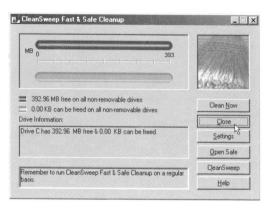

REMOVING UNWANTED INTERNET FILES

As you use the internet more and more, numerous files are created on your hard drive, which are in addition to the web pages that can be removed by using Fast & Safe Cleanup. These files are known as "cookies," and they contain records of websites you have visited and your preferences as determined by which parts of the website you clicked on. Internet cookies may also include a user ID if the site requires one. In the majority of cases, such files can be safely removed.

LAUNCHING CLEANSWEEP'S INTERNET OPTIONS

● To begin cleaning up the internet files on your hard drive, click on **Internet** on the left-hand side of the SystemWorks window.

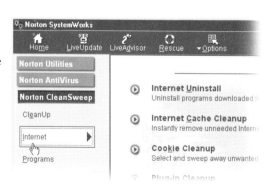

● Before being able to use the Cookie Cleanup option, you need to turn off a feature of Norton SystemWorks known as Safety Sweep. This feature is designed to prevent all but the most dispensable files from being deleted. Although Safety Sweep protects cookies (among other files), it is generally safe to remove cookies particularly when they begin to occupy valuable amounts of disk space.

● Click on **Options** in the menu bar and select **Norton CleanSweep**.

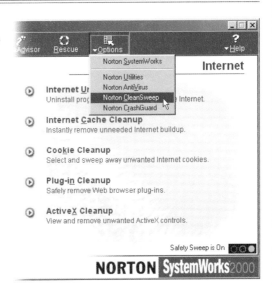

● In the **Options** dialog box, click in the **Off** radio button in the Safety Sweep panel toward the foot of the box.

● Click on **OK**.

Clicking this radio button turns Safety Sweep off

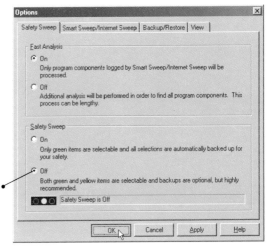

● The SystemWorks window now shows, at bottom right, that **Safety Sweep is Off**.

● Removing the cookies can be started by clicking on the **Cookie Cleanup** button panel.

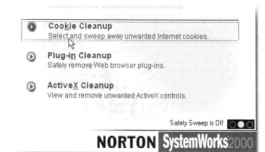

● In this example, the Cookie Cleanup dialog box shows a number of cookies on the hard drive. They can be selected individually by clicking in each check box. Alternatively, every entry can be selected by clicking on **Select All**.

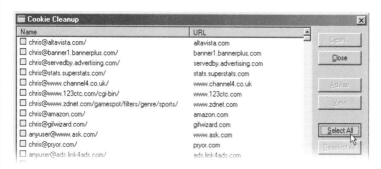

● Check marks now appear in the check boxes that are next to each of the cookies, which means they are now selected. Click on the **Clean** button at top right of the Cookie Cleanup window to begin the automatic process of removing the cookies.

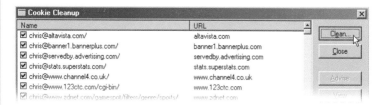

● You are asked if you wish to back up the files. However, the recommended default option is not to back them up and the reason is given in the window.

● Accept this default choice by clicking on **Next**.

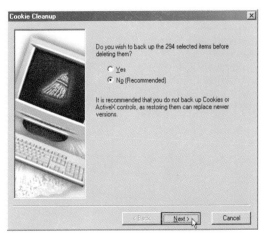

● You may wish to confirm the deletion of each item, particularly if there are a few cookies that you wish to keep. Not to confirm each deletion is the default option, which you can accept, again by clicking on **Next**.

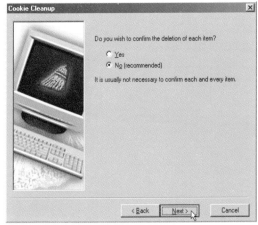

● Once you have made the selections offered by Cookie Cleanup, click on **Finish**.

The 294 selected files will be deleted, but not backed up.

Click Finish to delete the 294 selected files.

If you wish to view the summary of what will be deleted, click View.

● The deletions are carried out, and you are informed of the amount of data that has been removed.
● Click on **OK**.

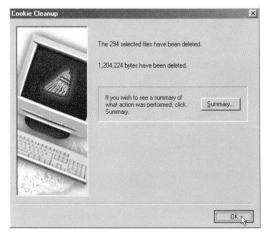

The 294 selected files have been deleted.

1,204,224 bytes have been deleted.

If you wish to see a summary of what action was performed, click Summary.

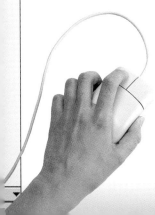

● The Cookie Cleanup dialog box reappears showing that there are no cookies left on the system.
● The last step is to click on **Close**. If you are a frequent user of the internet, it is advisable to clean up cookies regularly.

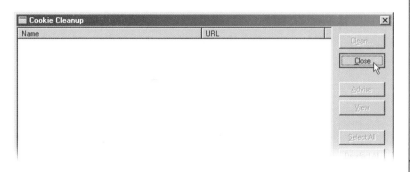

BACKING UP FILES

Norton SystemWorks contains a utility, called the Backup Wizard, which creates compressed backups of files to ensure that your most important programs and data files will be available should the originals be accidentally deleted.

LAUNCHING BACKUP WIZARD
● Click on **Programs** within Norton CleanSweep and click on the **Backup Wizard** button panel.

PERFORMING A BACKUP

● The Backup Wizard displays the programs contained on your computer in the same way as the Uninstall Wizard by using the contents of the **Start** menu ⬒. Access the program or file to be backed up by clicking on the plus sign next to **Programs** and scroll down the list until you find the program you want. In this example, a tool called Internet Tweak 2000 has been selected.

● Click on **Next** when you have made your own selection.

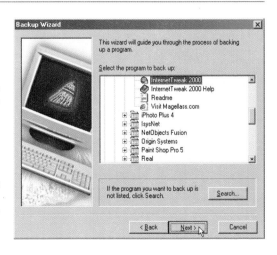

● The Backup Wizard suggests a location for the compressed backup and, unless you wish to change the location, click on **Next**.

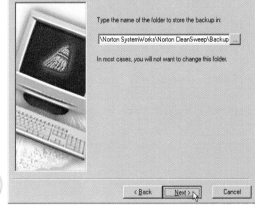

⬒ Uninstall
49 Wizard

● The following window
confirms the details that
have been selected and
gives the figure for the
amount of data that is to
be backed up.
● Click on **Finish** to
confirm that the backup
can begin.

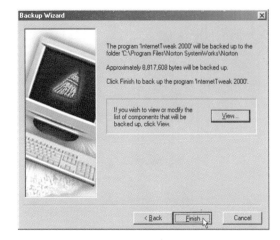

● A small panel is
displayed during the
backup process, and this
is rapidly replaced by a
window announcing that
the backup has been
successfully completed.
● Click on **OK** to end
the backup.

Transport Wizard
A common error in
using the Backup
Wizard is to create a
backup when you need
to move a program
from your desktop
computer to a laptop. In
these instances, always
use the Transport
Wizard to move files.

FREEZES AND CRASHES

Freezes and crashes are inevitable facts of computing life, but their damaging effects can be significantly reduced by using the features available in Norton CrashGuard.

NORTON FREEZECHECK

Without any protection from freezes or crashes, the usual choice is between closing the program or rebooting your system. Either course of action means that any unsaved data is lost.

Norton CrashGuard offers to provide that missing protection. Although CrashGuard cannot prevent software from occasionally going haywire, it can attempt to unfreeze an apparently frozen program.

LAUNCHING FREEZECHECK

● A freeze differs from a crash in that when a program becomes frozen, its window is still present on your monitor, but the program does not accept any commands that you issue. Any other software that you are running at the same time is usually working normally.

● When you suspect that a program has frozen, click on the **Norton CrashGuard** button in the Integrator.

● There are only two options within Norton CrashGuard. Click on the **FreezeCheck** button panel.

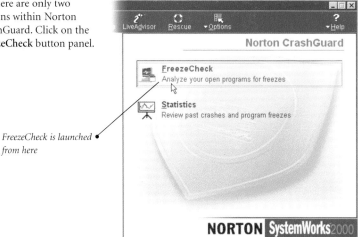

FreezeCheck is launched from here

● The FreezeCheck window opens in which you can scroll through a list of the different application that are currently running on your computer.
● Highlight the name of the apparently frozen application, and click on the **FreezeCheck** button.

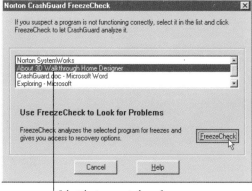

Select the program to be unfrozen

● The following window is known as **Norton CrashGuard Crash Assistant** for FreezeCheck. At the top of the window, FreezeCheck displays the name of the program, which in this case is About 3D Walkthrough Home Designer, and this is followed by FreezeCheck's diagnostic message, which here says that the program **Is Disabled**.

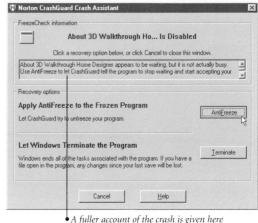

A fuller account of the crash is given here

● Below this is a scrolling text box that provides a fuller account of what FreezeCheck believes the situation to be along with a suggested course of action, which in this case is to click on a feature of FreezeCheck called **AntiFreeze**.

● The Norton AntiFreeze dialog box provides further information together with the opportunity to use **AntiFreeze** to unfreeze the program. Clicking on **Yes** is the most commonly used option unless you are severely warned otherwise.

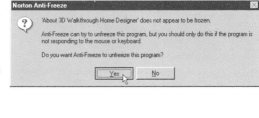

● Each piece of software is different, and within each one, a freeze can occur in several forms. Therefore, no typical freeze can be represented here. In this example, FreezeCheck has successfully opened the program's **Start Options** dialog box in which it has been possible to make corrections. Clicking on **OK** then successfully unfroze the program.

● It is highly advisable that once you have regained access to the program, you should save any work and restart the application to reduce the possibility of a further freeze.

Start Options

Memory for 3D View
◉ Enough for entire screen
◯ 1600 KByte

3D Pixel Size
◉ One Pixel
◯ 2 x 2 Pixel
◯ 4 x 4 Pixel

3D Pixel Colour Depth
◉ Hi Colour (=8 Bytes per 3D-Pixel)
◯ True Colour (=12 Bytes per 3D-Pixel)

Textures
☑ Use Mipmaps
Buffer memory for textures: 1024 KByte

Path for internal Objects
C:\WDesign\Internal   Browse...

Path for textures
C:\WDesign\Texture   Browse...

Catalogues
File : C:\WDesign\WDesign.LMK   Browse...
Base Path : C:\WDesign   Browse...

Ok   Cancel   Help

FREEZECHECK MESSAGES

FreezeCheck's messages depend on what it diagnoses. The messages that you may come across include:

The program is disabled.
Here you can wait for the program to finish a task, or click AntiFreeze to jump-start the program.

The program is not responding.
This message occurs when the program is not doing anything and appears to be waiting for input. AntiFreeze deals directly with the program and persuades it to begin responding again.

The program is not busy.
In this situation, the program may be expecting some input, and other parts of the program may be suspended until the input is received. AntiFreeze may be able to communicate with other parts of the program, which may not be anticipating any activity, and the results may be unpredictable. However, if little appears to be happening, AntiFreeze may be the best option.

The program appears ready.
No problems are detected, and the program appears to be working. Clicking on **Cancel** is the preferred option to return to the program and re-examine what is happening.

HANDLING CRASHES

Norton CrashGuard Crash Assistant can attempt to revive a stalled program, or possibly save your data if the program has irretrievably crashed. Because CrashGuard is constantly monitoring the behavior of your system and the software that it is running, crashes can be intercepted just as they are about to occur. Action can then be taken depending on the type and severity of the crash.

WHEN A CRASH HAPPENS
Because CrashGuard is constantly monitoring your programs and Windows while you are working, the first indication that you are likely to receive of a crash taking place is the sudden appearance on-screen of the Norton CrashGuard Crash Assistant window.

CRASHGUARD CRASH ASSISTANT

❶ Crash Information
The Crash Assistant's window is made up of several sections. The first is **Crash Information**, which gives you the name of the application that is experiencing problems.

❷ Program and System
The **Program and System** section contains icons indicating the severity of the crash. In this case, the **Program** icon shows a marginally fractured application window while the **System** icon contains a check mark, which means that the system-level software is still functioning normally.

❸ Crash Advisor
One of the most important parts of the Assistant's display is the **Crash Advisor**, which recommends what to do based on CrashGuard's analysis of the severity of the crash.

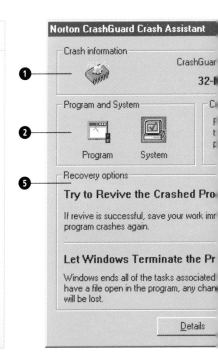

Enabling SafeOriginal

The SafeOriginal status is always shown in the Crash Assistant's window, and in this case it is **Enabled**. If the Crash Assistant shows that Safe-Original is Disabled, it can be turned on by first selecting **Norton CrashGuard** from **Options** in the menu bar of the Integrator. Click on the **SafeOriginal** tab and insert a check mark in the **Enable SafeOriginal** check box. Finally, click on **OK**.

CRASHGUARD CRASH ASSISTANT

❹ SafeOriginal

One specific danger of a crash is that the crashed program may attempt to overwrite the original data file with a corrupted version. If the Crash Assistant detects that this is happening, **SafeOriginal** creates a copy of the original file and places it in the SafeOriginal folder.

❺ Recovery options

The lower half of the Crash Assistant's window is devoted to the recovery options that CrashGuard considers to be the most appropriate for each individual crash. In this instance, the Assistant has provided two options:

Try to Revive the Crashed Program. This option appears when crashes may be partly recoverable. Clicking on **Revive** may return you to the application, but not every aspect of the program may be working normally. If you return to the application, you should try to save your data right away and then close the application.

Let Windows Terminate the Program, This option frequently appears in the Crash Assistant's list of recovery options. Clicking on this option will pass the control of your computer to the Windows operating system, which will close the program immediately. This is a quick method of returning your computer to normal functioning if you do not mind losing any data that you have not saved.

Given Crash Advisor's advice, clicking on **Revive** is the best option.

● Clicking **Revive** works immediately in some cases, but here, a further screen appears showing that CrashGuard can restart the program. Again, the advice of the Advisor should be followed by clicking on **Program**.

● You may be able to retrieve and save your data before closing and relaunching the program manually to prevent the problem from recurring.

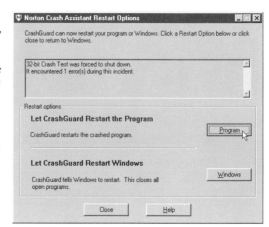

A FATAL CRASH

● For the purposes of comparison, an irrecoverable crash is illustrated here. The **Program and System** section of the Assistant's window shows a completely fractured application window, and the **System** icon represents a highly unstable operating system.

● The Crash Advisor recommends that **Terminate** is the best option and is the one that is selected here.

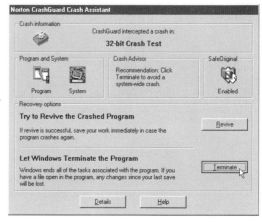

• The **Restart Options** window appears containing the option of restarting the program. However, as the Assistant indicated that the operating system has become unstable, the wisest course of action is to restart Windows – which amounts to rebooting your machine – by clicking on **Windows**.

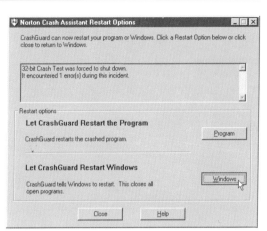

PROGRAM AND SYSTEM STATUS ICONS

The icons shown in the **Status indicators** panel of the Crash Assistant's window provide a quick, at-a-glance indication of how severe a crash you are experiencing in terms of both the program and Windows. The levels of severity are:

PROGRAM INDICATORS

 A crash has occurred, but you should be able to save your work by clicking on **Revive**.

 The program cannot be guaranteed to work and clicking on **Revive** may not retrieve your data.

 The program has crashed irretrievably. Clicking on **Revive** here may create further problems.

 The program is irretrievable. The **Terminate** option should be used and then reboot your system.

SYSTEM INDICATORS

 Windows is functioning normally and any other programs should not be affected.

 Windows has been affected by the program crash and rebooting your computer is the best option here.

GLOSSARY

APPLICATION
Another term for a piece of software, usually a program.

BROWSER
A browser is the program needed to view websites on the internet. When you select a website, the browser sends a request for the site to the web server where the website is stored and displays the page.

CACHE
A location on the hard drive where a web browser stores data (which can consist of text, graphics, and sounds) from websites that have been visited. When the sites are revisited, they are then downloaded more quickly and easily.

COOKIE
A piece of information unique to you that is saved on the hard drive by the web browser and contains information such as your user ID, personal preferences, and details of sites that you have visited.

CRASH
The term applied when a computer suddenly stops working during a routine operation. Typical signs of a crash include a "lockup," in which the PC appears to be running but will not allow any movement of the pointer or use of the keyboard.

DEFRAGMENTING
The process of reassembling and reorganizing program and data files that are badly distributed on a hard drive.

DOWNLOAD
The transfer of data from one computer to another. Your browser downloads HTML code and graphics to display a page.

FREEZE
When a program freezes, its window remains open, but does not respond to any instructions.

HARD DRIVE
Sometimes known as the hard disk, a large capacity primary drive used to store data.

HARDWARE
Hardware is the part of a computer that you can physically see or touch.

INSTALLING
The process of "loading" an item of software onto a hard drive. *See also* Uninstalling.

INTERNET
The network of interconnected computers that communicate by using agreed rules.

MODEM
A hardware device that enables computers to communicate via telephone lines.

OPERATING SYSTEM
Software that operates the computer. An operating system is the first program that loads and takes charge when you turn on your computer.

PERIPHERAL
A piece of equipment that can be connected to your computer and that is used for either input (a keyboard or scanner) or output (a printer or monitor).

PLUG-IN
A program that works in conjunction with web browsers to play audio and video.

RADIO BUTTON
An on-screen button in a program that turns on and off when clicked with a mouse.

REBOOT
Restarting a computer, usually by following an instruction when, for example, installing software, or by selecting Restart from the Shut Down options.

SOFTWARE
A computer needs software to function. Software ranges from simple utilities to immense computer games.

SYSTEM
A computer system as a whole, consisting of all the major components that make up the PC workstation.

UNINSTALLING
The process of removing an item of software from the hard drive by deleting all its files.

VIRUS
A program or piece of computer code deliberately created and distributed to destroy or disorganize data on other computer systems.

WEBSITE
A collection of web pages that are linked to one another, and sometimes to other websites.

WIZARD
A series of prompts to accomplish a specific task.

INDEX

ACKNOWLEDGMENTS

PUBLISHER'S ACKNOWLEDGMENTS

Dorling Kindersley would like to thank the following:

Symantec Corporation for kind permission to reproduce
screen shots of Norton SystemWorks 2000.

Every effort has been made to trace the copyright holders.
The publisher apologizes for any unintentional omissions and would be pleased,
in such cases, to place an acknowledgment in future editions of this book.

Norton AntiVirus™, Norton CleanSweep™, Norton CrashGuard™,
Norton Link Advisor™, Norton Utilities™, and Norton Web Services™
are registered trademarks of Symantec Corporation
in the US and/or other countries.